BREWITT

Discovering

BADGERS

Martin Banks

The Bookwright Press
New York · 1988

Discovering Nature

Further titles are in preparation

First published in the
United States in 1988 by
The Bookwright Press
387 Park Avenue South
New York, NY 10016

Library of Congress Cataloging-in-Publication Data

Banks, Martin, 1938–
   Discovering Badgers, by Martin Banks
      p. cm. — (Discovering nature.)
   Bibliography: p.
   Includes index.
   Summary: Explores the world of badgers, describing the
different types in Europe, America, and Asia and their habits
and habitats.
   ISBN 0–531–18225–8
   1. Badgers — Juvenile literature. (1. Badgers.) I. Title.
II. Series.
QL737.C25B26   1989
599.74′447 — dc19
                            88–5071
                            CIP
                            AC

Cover *The Eurasian badger is found throughout Europe and Asia, down to southern China.*

Frontispiece *A six-month-old Eurasian badger cub running across the South Downs in Sussex, England.*

First published in 1988 by
Wayland (Publishers) Limited
61 Western Road, Hove
East Sussex BN3 1JD, England

Typeset by DP Press Ltd., Sevenoaks, Kent
Printed in Italy by Sagdos S.p.A., Milan

Contents

1
Introducing Badgers

The Eurasian badger has distinctive black and white stripes running down its head and face.

What Are Badgers?

Badgers are medium-sized **mammals** with a squat, bear-like appearance. They are members of the **mustelid** family, a group of animals that includes otters, weasels, skunks and polecats. Like badgers, these animals possess scent **glands** at the base of the tail.

Badgers are found living in many parts of the world. There are different species in Europe and Asia, one in North America and one in Africa. But there are no badgers in South America or Australia.

There are nine species of badgers altogether. All of them have similar habits, but the honey badger, or ratel, which lives in Africa and Asia, is not closely related to the others.

Badgers are very powerful creatures. Most of them are powerful diggers. They use their strong front legs and feet to excavate burrows in which they live. The word badger may have come from a French word *becheur*, which means "digger." Some badgers have very distinctive markings on the face or head.

The Eurasian species has black stripes running down its head and face, and the American badger has similar, less bold markings on its face.

Badgers vary in size. Among the largest are the Eurasian (or European), American and hog badgers. An adult Eurasian badger may be nearly a yard long, and weigh over 12 kg (26 lb). The smallest badgers live in Asia. These are the ferret badgers. They are more lightly built and are the only badgers to have long tails. An adult ferret badger is about 50 cm (20 in) in length, with a weight of 2 kg (4.4 lb).

The American badger is found throughout the drier regions of the United States.

The Body of a Badger

Badgers are squat, thickset animals, with powerful, wedge-shaped bodies, small heads, thick necks and short legs and tails. Ferret badgers, with long tails and lighter build, do not resemble other badgers so closely. A badger's body is covered with thick, coarse hair and extremely tough skin. In most species, the hair is a mixture of brown, black or gray mixed with white. In some species, like the honey badger, the body has a distinct pattern of markings.

Their claws are used for digging burrows and scratching out food from the earth.

A badger has a broad, bear-like head, with small ears and eyes. The muzzle is long, and the nose is prominent. Badgers rely chiefly on their strong sense of smell to find food and to detect danger.

A badger's feet are broad and flat, like a bear's. Both front and hind feet have five toes with long curved claws.

Badgers are **omnivores**. **Fossil** remains show that the early badgers, which were present some four million years ago, had teeth that were more suitable for a **carnivorous** diet. Today's badgers still eat meat, but their teeth have changed. They now have flatter **molars** and smaller, blunter **canines**. But the honey badger is still able to catch and kill animals up to the size of young antelope, while the American badger

THE BODY OF A BADGER

ears

muzzle

non-retractable
claws

foreleg

hindleg

tail

eats a larger proportion of small rodents, like rabbits and mice, than do other badgers.

Like other mustelids, badgers have scent glands under the base of their short bushy tail. Badgers use them to produce a strong-smelling scent. This is used to help badgers identify each other. Some species, like the Asian stink badgers, can produce a foul-smelling liquid which they squirt at their enemies as a means of defense.

2
Where Badgers Live

Badgers usually like to live in woodlands where there is plenty of cover and a good supply of food.

Woodlands and Grasslands

Badgers live in a wide variety of **habitats**. Most prefer woodlands and grasslands but they are able to live in other places too. The Asian badgers usually live in jungle or thick grassland where there is plenty of cover. The honey badger, which is found in many parts of Africa and Asia, lives in thick forest, light woodlands and grasslands, and even semi-desert areas.

The North American badger is found in an equally wide variety of habitats. It lives in woodlands, open plains, farmland and in mountainous regions. American badgers are even quite at home in the hot deserts of Mexico and Arizona.

Badgers have two main requirements for survival. One is a suitable supply of food. The other requirement is ground that is soft enough for them to dig in, because most badgers like to live and sleep underground in a comfortable and safe retreat.

The Eurasian, or European, badger lives in Europe and Asia. In Britain, it can be found in almost every type of habitat, from sea level to high up on hillsides and mountains. The largest numbers of badgers live in woodlands surrounded by fields and pastureland. That is because trees provide ideal shelter, and badgers can obtain a good supply of food both in the woods and in the fields.

But European badgers can also live quite successfully on sea cliffs, moorland and other exposed places. In all of these places they can find food and dig burrows. However, badgers rarely live in flat, marshy areas, which are likely to become flooded. Although they may forage in a marsh, they will dig their burrows in the nearest area of higher ground where they are safe from flooding.

The honey badger, or ratel, excavates a burrow in a dry, sandy area of Namibia in southern Africa.

Burrows and Setts

Badgers are natural diggers. All of them spend considerable parts of their lives underground, though the small ferret badgers of Asia climb and sometimes rest in trees. Other badgers normally rest underground, in tunnels that they excavate themselves. A badger digs using powerful strokes of its strong front feet and claws. Then it kicks the soil away from the entrance with its hind legs. Sometimes a badger enlarges a natural hole under tree roots or rocks, making the hole longer and deeper to suit its needs. Rabbit holes are often used in this way.

The Eurasian badger is perhaps the most expert digger of all. This species lives in family groups that consist of up to ten or more animals. Eurasian badgers dig long, complicated networks of tunnels, with inter-connecting chambers where they rest and sleep. These tunnel systems are called setts, or burrows.

Badgers usually prefer to dig their setts in sloping, well-drained hillsides. Sandy or loamy soils make the digging easier. Heavy soils like clay, which are harder to dig and become waterlogged

Unlike the Eurasian badger, the American badger does not use the same burrow year after year but often digs a new one.

easily, are not favored by badgers. On a hillside, several badger setts will often be found at roughly the same height above sea level. This is where a band of a soft or sandy soil is

Badgers prefer to dig their burrows in well-drained, sandy soil.

sandwiched in between others in which the badgers find it less easy to dig.

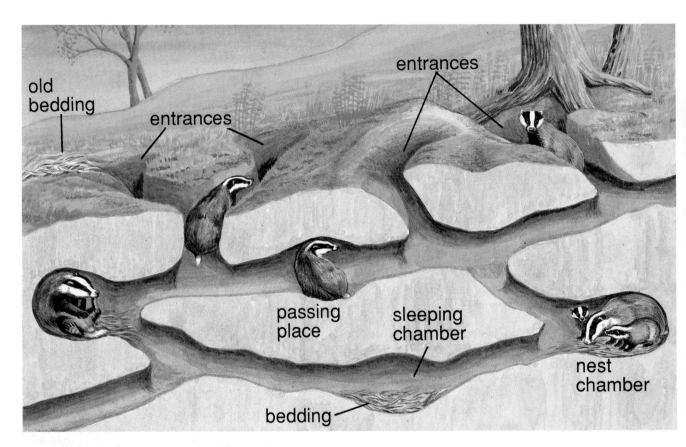

old bedding

entrances

entrances

passing place

sleeping chamber

nest chamber

bedding

Inside a Sett

The setts of European badgers may be very ancient structures. Some of them are believed to be hundreds of years old. They have been lived in by many different generations of badgers since they were first dug. The older setts are often very large. The tunnels may extend many yards into the hillside. At intervals the tunnels open out into chambers. Here badgers sleep and rest during the daytime. Usually, the chambers are lined with bracken or grass, which the badgers collect from the surrounding countryside. This is dragged to the sett itself and taken down the holes. Every so often, badgers have a "spring cleaning," removing the old bedding from the burrow and bringing in fresh. This may happen at any time of year. Sometimes piles of old bedding lie on the earth platforms outside a badger's burrow.

Large badger setts contain many entrance holes. They may not all be used by the badgers at any one time. Smaller setts have fewer entrances; some have only one or two.

Badger setts are easily identified by the large mounds of earth in front of the entrances. These are what the badgers have removed in the course of their digging. As the badgers extend their tunnels and dig deeper into the hillsides, the mounds of earth they bring to the surface get larger. At large burrows that are very old, these piles of earth resemble huge platforms, trampled hard by the feet of many resident badgers.

Several badger families may reside in one wood. When this happens, the area is divided into **territories**. Each family will use one large sett at the center of its territory and may live in one or more other smaller setts as well.

A badger collecting leaves for bedding to line the chambers of its den.

Sharing a Sett

Badgers' tunnels are very attractive to some other animals too. As long as they do not mind the badgers, they are saved the work of digging their own homes. In Europe, foxes will sometimes live in a badger's sett, even though the two species do not seem very friendly. The badgers seem to tolerate the presence of the fox, but the fox is careful to use a part of the sett that the badgers are not using. It usually comes and goes by one of the entrances not used by badgers. Sometimes, a vixen (a female fox) will rear her cubs in a badger's sett, while badger cubs are growing up in another part of it.

The American badger also digs long tunnels. The abandoned tunnels make good homes for coyotes, which live in the same areas as the badgers. Empty badger setts are often used by rabbits too. In some areas, rabbits may even live in an occupied sett. It can be a risky business, for badgers eat rabbits when they can catch them. Probably the rabbits live in a part of

This is a typical entrance to a sett – it is on sloping ground in woodland with a mound of freshly dug earth outside.

the burrow away from the resident badgers.

Occasionally, badgers are found living above ground, in nests that they build for themselves. Even more rarely, a female badger has been

A badger comes out of its hole at night to search for food.

known to rear her cubs away from the safety of a burrow, but that is very unusual.

3
On The Move

Badgers are seldom seen in daylight except in quiet places and will return to the den at the first hint of danger.

Coming Above Ground

Badgers are **nocturnal**. They spend the hours of daylight sleeping underground. If they are undisturbed, some species, such as American and Eurasian badgers, are active in the daytime too. The honey badger is another species that moves around and hunts in the daytime. In Britain, badgers usually emerge at dusk or after dark. But during the summer months, when the nights are short, they may come above ground well before sunset.

When a badger comes to the entrance of its burrow, it pauses for a while. It will sniff the air and listen intently, possibly for several minutes. Badgers have poor eyesight. They rely on their hearing and excellent sense of smell to detect danger. Only when the badger is satisfied there is no danger will it come out. Even then, the least hint of danger may make it bolt underground again. Then it may wait a long time before coming to the entrance once more.

When a badger first comes above ground, it usually has a good scratch. Badgers are clean animals and do not tolerate fleas. Scratching in the confined space of the underground chambers may be difficult. So the animal makes up for it when it emerges at night. The Eurasian badger often sits or lies on its haunches, rather like a panda or a bear, while it nibbles the fur on its belly with its teeth or scratches with its claws. But badgers normally move on all fours, never on two legs like bears.

Badgers use their teeth and claws to get rid of the fleas and other insects that live inside their underground chambers.

Foothpaths and Trails

Badgers often move along clearly defined trails and paths when they are above ground. These paths lead from the burrow or sett to their feeding grounds. Moving along the same routes, night after night, badgers create well-worn paths through the vegetation. These paths are often clearly visible around a badger's sett and lead away from it in different directions.

A badger's front feet turn inward slightly, and badgers walk on the soles of their feet as well as their toes. A badger walks slowly when it is searching for food, stopping to eat or snuffle in the grass and then moving on. When a badger is in a hurry, it

Because of their heavy bodies and short legs, badgers tend to move slowly on land. Here an American badger swims across a lake.

moves at a quick, lumbering trot. Badgers can be quite noisy when they move through the vegetation. Every so often they pause to listen for danger before moving on again. Badgers can move fast, too. When frightened, a badger uses a bounding gallop to get back to the safety of its burrow as soon as it can.

Some badgers can climb. The ferret badgers of Asia are the only ones that climb trees. But occasionally, Eurasian badgers will clamber a few feet up a sloping tree trunk. Badger cubs frequently play on logs and tree stumps. Badger paths sometimes lead up very steep banks and over stone walls. This shows that despite its heavy, low-slung body, a badger can climb quite well when it wants to.

Cubs will often climb over tree stumps and logs in play. The dead wood can also be a good source of food, such as insects.

4
Food and Feeding

The honey badger, or ratel, eats many small animals. This one has caught and killed a python.

What Badgers Eat

Badgers are omnivores. Like most animals with an omnivorous diet, badgers eat many different kinds of food. Most eat a wide assortment of plant foods, including seeds and fruits, bulbs, roots and grasses. They also eat beetles, slugs, snails, and particularly earthworms. Especially in spring and autumn, earthworms are among the main foods of the Eurasian badger. On damp nights a badger can catch and eat several hundred earthworms in just a few hours.

American badgers eat gophers, ground squirrels and ground-nesting birds such as pheasants. Eurasian badgers also eat birds' eggs and small rodents like mice and voles as well as young rabbits. Badgers dig these animals out of their holes.

Two species, the American badger and the honey badger, are more carnivorous than other badgers. A honey badger can catch and kill animals up to the size of young antelopes. It also eats snakes, lizards and even porcupines, but its name gives a clue to one of its favorite foods. Honey badgers frequently rob the nests of wild bees to feed on the honeycombs. Other badgers, too, break into nests of wasps and bees when they can find them.

A honey badger carries a piece of fresh honeycomb from a beehive.

Finding Their Food

Badgers are **foragers**, moving slowly along and eating almost anything edible that they find on the way. A lot of food is found by smell; the badger pushes its snout into the grass, and then digs down to unearth roots or insects. Badgers, especially European badgers, go searching for earthworms in pastureland, in damp conditions when worms are more likely to be near the surface. When a badger discovers a worm, it grabs it with its teeth and pulls it out. If the worm

The hog badger forages for grubs and insects with its long, pig-like snout.

breaks, the badger will quickly dig out the remains. Fields where a badger has been foraging for worms on a damp day may be covered with freshly dug holes.

The hog badger of Asia has, as its name suggests, a nose rather like that of a pig, and when searching for worms, bulbs and insects it uses the snout the way a pig does, to root up the ground.

A badger's diet is very varied. It will eat almost anything edible that it can find.

Many badgers change their diet according to the season. The Eurasian badger eats lots of earthworms in spring and summer. It is more likely to find birds' eggs and young mammals at this time too. Fruits, cereals and nuts are eaten in autumn, while insects, roots and bulbs may be eaten at any time of year.

The honey badger has a remarkable way of finding bees' nests. Sometimes it is led to a nest by a small bird called the honey guide. Honey guides like honey too, but they cannot break open a bees' nest. So the bird goes in search of a honey badger. If it finds one, it calls and displays to attract the badgers' attention, then leads it back to the nest. The badger breaks the nest open and feeds on the honey, taking little notice of the angry bees. The honey guide gets its share of honey too.

5
Family Life

Eurasian badgers like the company of other badgers and usually live in large groups, which share the same sett.

Living Alone and Living Together

Badgers can be either **social** or **solitary** animals. The American badger and the honey badger are usually found living on their own. The badgers of Southeast Asia are normally solitary animals too.

The Eurasian badger is a social animal. It lives in groups, which are sometimes called clans. A group of badgers usually consists of an adult male and one or more adult females with young of different ages. Male Eurasian badgers are called boars, and the females, sows. Each group of badgers occupies its own sett. Some large groups may live in one sett most of the time, but occasionally will move into a smaller sett nearby. This will happen if they are disturbed.

A group of badgers has its own territory, which varies considerably in size, depending on the habitat.

Woodlands, which provide plenty of food and cover, can support a large badger population. This will consist of several groups, each living in an area of about 40 acres. Within this area, badgers from other groups are unwelcome. Members of a group mark the edges of their territory with scent. They also dig special pits where they leave their droppings. These latrines, which are found close to the sett and along the boundaries, are also used to show the badgers' ownership of a territory.

Badgers in a group also mark each other with their scent. It helps them identify members of their group, particularly when they meet away from the sett. If a resident badger meets one with an unfamiliar scent, the stranger is likely to be attacked and chased away.

Open areas like prairies have fewer badgers living in them. The territory of each group will be much larger, for food is not as plentiful. The boundaries will probably not be so well marked because there is less chance that other badgers will trespass.

Badgers mark the other members of their group and the boundaries of their territory with scent from their anal scent glands.

Mating and Giving Birth

A male badger learns when a female is ready to breed from the scent marks she leaves. Some badgers only come together for **mating**. Other species live for part of the time in pairs, while the Eurasian badger lives in groups

The mother stays underground in the nest until the cubs are a few weeks old.

throughout the year.

Eurasian badgers mate in almost any month of the year. But the cubs are almost always born in the spring. Badgers have a variable time of

pregnancy. Although the female's eggs are fertilized after mating, they usually do not begin to develop for several months. This is called delayed implantation. After the eggs have begun to develop normally, the cubs will be born after a **gestation** period of about two months.

In Britain and Europe, badger cubs are usually born between February and May. The female retires to a quiet chamber in the sett before the birth. She then brings in quantities of bracken and dry grass with which to line the nest.

Badger cubs are blind and helpless at birth. There are from one to four cubs in a litter, with two or three being the most common number. For several weeks they remain in the warmth of their nest. Here the mother suckles them. At night, she leaves them for short periods while she goes off in search of food.

In the top picture these cubs are three weeks old. By five weeks (below) they look more like badgers.

Growing Up

When the cubs are several days old, their eyes begin to open. At two months, they are well developed. Their baby coats are silvery gray in color, but the black and white striped head already looks like an

A badger keeps its cub in line with a sharp tug on its tail.

adult's head. The cubs will already have explored the tunnels and chambers in the sett. Soon they are ready to come above ground. The mother may wait for fine weather before taking them outside of the sett. For the first few evenings she will be very cautious, testing the air for any sign of danger before allowing the cubs to come out. The baby badgers are still unsure on their legs and stay close to the entrance of the sett to begin with.

As they get older, the cubs become more adventurous. They start to explore farther away from the sett entrance. They play energetic games, chasing and wrestling with each other. Often, the fur on their bodies is raised, showing how excited they are. Though the male badger lives with the family, he takes only a small amount of interest in the cubs. At dusk, he is often the first to emerge from the sett,

but he is likely to go off in search of food, leaving the mother and cubs to follow later.

Badger cubs emerge from their dens in spring when there is plenty of food. They soon learn to forage for themselves.

An adult badger leads a party of cubs on a nighttime expedition to find food. At first they do not venture far from the lair.

Within a few weeks of coming above ground, the cubs begin to forage for themselves. Following the adults on their nightly feeding sessions, they learn the best places to find food. By autumn, they are well grown and not much smaller than the adults. During the winter months, Eurasian badgers may stay underground for several days if the weather is very bad. But they do not **hibernate**, and they remain active all through the winter.

Badger cubs normally leave their parents in the autumn. They move to a nearby sett, while the parents prepare for the birth of new cubs next spring. But if the sett is very large, the older cubs may continue living in another part of it. Badgers become full-grown during their second year and normally produce their first cubs in the following spring.

Other species of badgers probably rear their young in the same way as the Eurasian badger, but that is the only one that has been closely studied so far. A lot more is known about its habits than those of other species.

A sow badger gives her cub a thorough grooming.

6
Enemies and Survival

Except for the fierce honey badger, badgers are generally timid, harmless animals that avoid people if they can.

Badgers and People

Badgers have a long association with people. In Britain, the old name for a badger, "Brock," appears at the beginning of several village and place names. It shows that badgers lived nearby when these places acquired their names.

Most badgers are shy, harmless creatures that avoid people if possible. However, the honey badger has a reputation for being very fierce. Sometimes it will attack people, and even vehicles, for no apparent reason. Even much larger animals such as lions avoid meeting a honey badger if they can.

"Badger baiting" was once considered a sport. The badgers were dug out of their setts and several dogs were pitted against one badger. This very cruel practice, which involved suffering for both dogs and the

badger, is now illegal. But unfortunately, badgers and badger setts are still disturbed in some parts of the world by people who carry on badger digging in secret.

Badgers may get hit by cars and trucks, particularly when they cross main roads and highways. At night, caught in the glare of headlights, the animals are too slow to escape. In

A scent trail is laid to lead badgers into the new tunnel under a busy road.

countries like Britain, where there are many badgers, special tunnels are sometimes designed for badgers to use. When an old badger path crosses a new road, they soon learn to use the tunnel instead, and the lives of many badgers are saved.

Badgers and Other Animals

In many countries badgers do a lot of good, ridding farmland of pests such as slugs and beetles that are harmful to crops. In forestry plantations

The Malaysian stink badger squirts its foul-smelling liquid at an attacking wild dog.

badgers are welcome, since they help to keep down the numbers of voles and rabbits, which damage young trees by gnawing at their bark.

Badgers have few natural enemies. They can defend themselves against almost any attack, since they have tough skins, sharp claws and strong teeth. Some badgers have other defenses too. They can squirt a foul-smelling liquid from their scent glands at an attacker. If this goes in the eyes, it can cause blindness. The stink badger of Malaysia is named after the unpleasant smell of its scent glands.

Although badgers have few natural enemies, some species are hunted for their skins. The stiff bristles of American and Eurasian badgers are ideal for making shaving or paint brushes. The stink badger, or teledu, is hunted by the natives of Southeast Asia, both for meat and for the contents of its scent glands, which are used in the manufacture of perfume.

In Britain, there is a relationship between badgers and domestic cattle that is not yet fully understood. Some badgers in Britain are known to carry a disease called bovine tuberculosis. It seems the badgers first caught it from infected cows, by feeding around cow dung. In some areas, whole badger colonies have been killed to try to prevent this disease from spreading. But some people think that badgers do not pass the disease back to cattle, and, therefore, it is unnecessary to kill them.

A badger has been poisoned in an attempt to stop the spread of bovine tuberculosis.

Are Badgers Pests?

Sometimes badgers are thought of as pests by country-dwelling people, believed to kill and eat young lambs and chickens. But there are very few cases where a badger has been proved to be the culprit. Very occasionally a rogue badger may kill poultry, but it

Young badgers are sometimes considered pests by farmers because they trample growing crops when they play in fields.

seems likely that where a badger has been found eating a lamb, the lamb was already dead when the badger discovered it.

Badgers, especially European badgers, sometimes become unpopular with farmers because of their digging habits. If a sett is excavated at the edge of a field, some of the holes may be in the field itself. That can make driving a tractor or other farm machinery dangerous. In spring and summer, young badgers sometimes damage growing crops. If they play regularly in a wheatfield, their pathways will soon begin to flatten the crop over quite a large area. This means it cannot be harvested.

Badgers living near the edge of towns have occasionally been known to raid garbage cans in search of food, but badgers in general are not regarded as being harmful animals. In Britain, badgers are protected by

special laws, which make it an offense to injure or kill them except in special circumstances.

In Britain, foxes are usually blamed for overturned garbage cans but badgers are often the culprits.

7
Looking for Badgers

A watcher must keep absolutely still and quiet in order to observe badgers at close range.

Badgers are normally active at night, so you need to go out in the evening, or very early in the morning to see them, but you can look for their burrows in the daytime. American badgers are found in the plains, prairies and deserts of the West, from southwestern Canada to central Mexico. European badgers are easier to watch because they are sometimes found living in parks and open spaces in towns as well as woodlands on the outskirts of cities.

To watch badgers, first make sure the burrow or sett is occupied. Look for fresh paths, footprints and freshly dug latrines. Try placing some sticks carefully in front of the holes. If they have been moved by the next day, you will know the badgers are there.

Spring and summer are the best times for watching badgers. Wear dark, warm clothes and take a flashlight. Choose a comfortable place

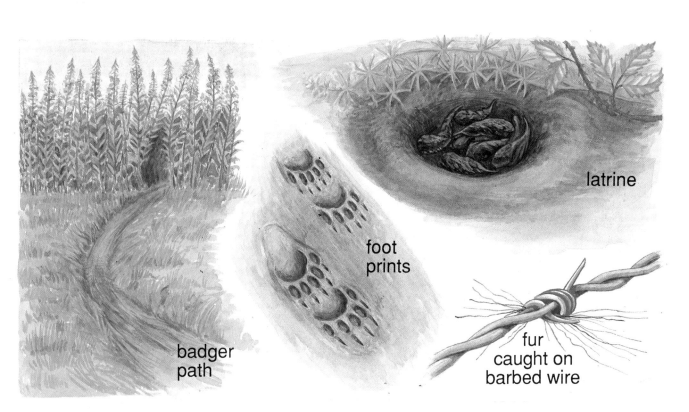

badger
path

foot
prints

latrine

fur
caught on
barbed wire

to stand or sit, several yards away from the holes. Remember that any wind should be blowing from the sett to you, and not the other way around.

Spreading food such as nuts and raisins around the entrances to the sett or burrow will encourage the badgers to stay in view longer before

The signs that badgers are around.

they move away to look for food. Badger watching is an enjoyable and rewarding pastime. But remember that the less you disturb the badgers, the more chance you will have of seeing them again on another visit.

Glossary

Canine(s) Sharp pointed teeth (two in upper jaw and two in lower jaw) that are used for biting and tearing food.

Carnivore Animal that eats meat and has teeth designed for tearing flesh.

Forage To move about in search of food.

Fossil Remains of an animal, such as its bones or tracks, which have been preserved in rocks over millions of years.

Gestation The period between mating and birth when the young are developing inside the mother.

Glands Parts of the body that produce special substances, such as musk or scent.

Habitat The type of country where an animal or plant is normally found.

Hibernate To spend the coldest months of the year in a state of reduced activity. May last several weeks or months. Hibernating animals do not feed and their heart and breathing rate become slow.

Mammal Warm-blooded animals that feed their young on milk and have hair or fur.

Mating The act by which male and female animals join together to produce young.

Molars The large cheek teeth that are used for crushing and grinding up food.

Mustelid Member of a group of mammals that have scent glands at the root of the tail. Polecats, weasels, otters and skunks, as well as badgers, are mustelids.

Nocturnal Active by night. Nocturnal animals sleep in the daytime and become active at night.

Omnivore An animal that eats both meat and plant food – its diet usually includes anything edible.

Pregnancy The time when a female animal is carrying her unborn young in her body.

Social Habitually living in groups rather than alone.

Solitary Habitually living alone.

Territory The area where an animal, or group of animals, lives. Animals may defend their territories against others of the same species.

Finding Out More

The following books will give you more information about badgers:

Animal Homes by Malcolm Penny. The Bookwright Press, 1987.
The Badger by Carl R. Green and William Sanford. Crestwood House, 1986.
Wonders of Badgers by Sigmund A. Lavine. Dodd, Mead, 1985.
The Year of the Badger by Molly Burkett. Lippincott, 1974.

Index

Picture Acknowledgments

Biofotos: Heather Angel 18, Geoffrey Kinns 39, 42; Bruce Coleman: 9, Robert P. Carr 14, Leonard Lee Rue 15, Peter Hinchliffe 19, 20, 32, 34, 35, Jen & Des Bartlett 22, C.B. & D.W. Frith 26, Hans Reinhard 28, Jane Burton 33; Frank Lane: R.P. Lawrence 10, Martin B. Withers 21, 23, 27, 29, 31 (top & bottom), 40, M. Clark 37; OSF: Robin Redfern 17, Alastair Shay 41; Survival Anglia: John Lynch frontispiece, Joe B. Blossom 12, Jen & Des Bartlett 13, 24, Lee Lyon 25, Marianne Wilding 30, 36; Zefa: H. Reinhard Cover, 8. Illustrations are by Wendy Meadway.